CIVIL LIBERTIES

Essential Viewpoints

CIVIL
LIBERTIES

BY SCOTT GILLAM

Content Consultant
Eric W. Mogren, J.D., Ph.D.
Associate Professor, History
Northern Illinois University

ABDO
Publishing Company

CREDITS

Published by ABDO Publishing Company, 8000 West 78th Street, Edina, Minnesota 55439. Copyright © 2008 by Abdo Consulting Group, Inc. International copyrights reserved in all countries. No part of this book may be reproduced in any form without written permission from the publisher. The Essential Library™ is a trademark and logo of ABDO Publishing Company.

Printed in the United States.

Editor: Rebecca Rowell
Cover Design: Becky Daum
Interior Design: Lindaanne Donohoe

Library of Congress Cataloging-in-Publication Data
Gillam, Scott.
  Civil liberties / Scott Gillam.
    p. cm.—(Essential viewpoints)
  Includes bibliographical references and index.
  ISBN 978-1-59928-858-1
  1. Civil rights—United States—Juvenile literature. I. Title.

JC599.U5G527 2008
323.0973—dc22

                    2007013878

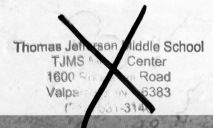

TABLE OF CONTENTS

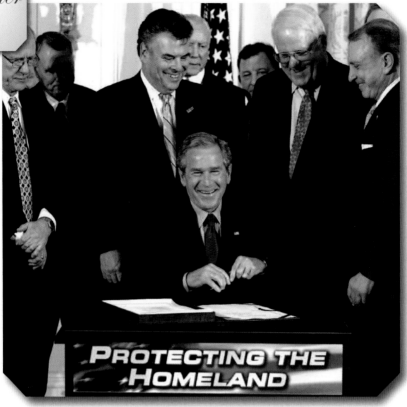

PROTECTING THE
HOMELAND

*President Bush, center, signs the USA Patriot Terrorism Prevention
Reauthorization Act of 2005 on March 9, 2006.*

GOVERNMENT POWER AND
CIVIL LIBERTIES

*I*magine a newspaper not being able to
report the news as it happened or was
witnessed. Instead, the government tells the newspaper
what to print. Picture being jailed for a month without
knowing what crime you were accused of committing.

Think about what it would be like if government or military personnel entered people's homes and went through their belongings at any time, without any warning, and without giving any reason. The laws of the United States prevent such things from happening.

The United States is both admired and despised for its system of government. The U.S. government is a democracy—government by the people. Citizens elect representatives, or leaders, who establish laws on their behalf. Election victories are generally decided by majority rule.

A democracy is only one type of government. Other types of government include totalitarian and monarchical systems. The key difference between various types of government is the amount of power citizens have and how leaders and laws are determined. For example, while U.S. citizens help choose political

Types of Government

There are several types of government. Examples include:

- The United Kingdom is a constitutional monarchy. The government consists of a monarch, currently Queen Elizabeth II, and Parliament.

- Cuba is a totalitarian state, which means there is only one political party: communist. As a totalitarian state, citizens must do what the government says and they are not allowed to leave the country.

- The United States of America is a democracy. It is also a federal republic, which means that there are a number of self-governing states (in this case, 50) that are united by a central government.

leaders, individuals in Cuba, which has a totalitarian government, do not elect those in power or influence the laws that are put into place.

In order to work well, every government must have some power over its citizens. In return for submitting to the government's power, citizens receive benefits. In the United States, the government determines how much money residents must pay in taxes. The government also has a great deal of power in deciding how this money is spent. For instance, taxes can

Amending the Constitution

The Bill of Rights lists the first 10 amendments to the U.S. Constitution. Since the initial 10 amendements were ratified, or approved, several additional amendments have been proposed. Some of the proposed amendments have been ratified, some have not. Currently, there are are 27 amendments.

There are two ways to propose an amendment:

- A bill passes by a two-thirds majority in both the Senate and the House of Representatives. All current amendments were proposed in this manner.

- A national Constitutional Convention is called by two-thirds of the states' legislatures, which proposes one or more amendments. This method of proposal has never been used.

To be ratified, a proposed amendment must be accepted by three-fourths of the states. This may be done by state legislatures or by state conventions. The method for ratification may be specified by the proposed amendment. If the method is not specified, amendments automatically go to state legislatures. Proposal by Congress followed by ratification by state conventions has happened once. All other amendments were proposed by Congress and then ratified by state legislatures.

go toward improving roads, providing services such as public transportation and health care, or funding the military. In general, U.S. citizens accept the government's power to spend their tax dollars. And if they do not accept it, their democratic system gives them the opportunity to change spending decisions through the election process. In addition, civil liberties give citizens the opportunity to express their dissatisfaction freely, without concern for punishment.

CIVIL LIBERTIES

Liberty is the right of an individual to act as one chooses. Civil liberties are those freedoms protected by a nation's laws or constitution. Examples of civil liberties include freedom of religion and freedom of speech. These freedoms allow citizens to worship as they wish and to speak their minds freely and without fear of persecution. Civil liberties exist to

The Declaration of Independence

The colonies officially separated from England with the Declaration of Independence. Written between June 11 and June 28, 1776, the document lists grievances against the king of England and notes Thomas Jefferson's thoughts on "self-evident truths":

"... We hold these truths to be self-evident, that all men are created equal, that they are endowed by their Creator with certain unalienable Rights, that among these are Life, Liberty and the pursuit of Happiness.— That to secure these rights, Governments are instituted among Men, deriving their just powers from the consent of the governed,—That whenever any Form of Government becomes destructive of these ends, it is the Right of the People to alter or to abolish it, and to institute new Government, laying its foundation on such principles and organizing its powers in such form, as to them shall seem most likely to effect their Safety and Happiness. ..."[1]

The U.S. Bill of Rights

limit the power of the government to control or dictate the actions of the individual. In the 1700s, after the United States gained independence from England, the framers of the U.S. Constitution added the Bill of Rights to ensure civil liberties.

THE BILL OF RIGHTS

When creating the Constitution, the founding fathers established the basic laws of the federal government. To prevent any abuse of government power, these men then created the Bill of Rights to address the rights of individual citizens. The Bill of Rights is the first ten amendments to the Constitution. They detail a variety of human rights or freedoms:

- Amendment I addresses what many people consider the most fundamental of freedoms: religion, speech, and the press. This amendment also provides for the right to assemble and to petition the government.

- Amendment II provides the right to keep and bear arms.

- Amendment III prevents the housing of military personnel in citizens' homes.

- Amendment IV protects against the government

searching or taking individuals' property or belongings without a good reason.

- Amendment V addresses the justice system, including due process (all rights of the accused must be upheld), double jeopardy (a person cannot be tried a second time for the same crime), and self-incrimination (a person cannot "in any criminal case to be a witness against himself"). In addition, this amendment states that a person's property cannot "be taken for public use, without just compensation."[2]

- Amendment VI also addresses the justice system, explaining what goes into providing a fair trial. Specifically, it details a speedy and public trial that is decided by a jury. In addition, the accused has the right to be informed of the crime of which they are accused, "to be confronted with the witnesses against him," to get "witnesses in his favor," and "to have the Assistance of Counsel for his defense."[3]

- Amendment VII provides for civil trials by jury.

- Amendment VIII prohibits excessive bail and fines, as well as the use of cruel and unusual punishment.

- Amendment IX protects the rights that are not specifically addressed in the Bill of Rights.

- Amendment X gives the powers not granted to the federal government by the U.S. Constitution and not prohibited by the Constitution to the individual states go or the people. In other words, these rights are retained by the states and the people rather than by the federal government.

The Heart of the Controversy

How important are such rights? Are there times when these rights should be limited, such as when terrorists are said to threaten the United States and its allies? Are there people to whom these rights should not apply? For example, when the U.S. military questions a suspected enemy, should interrogation techniques that might be considered cruel and unusual be allowed? Should the government be allowed to listen to individuals' private conversations or read their personal correspondence on the chance it may uncover a plan to attack the United States or its citizens? Should the president be

"A bad constitution brings civic turmoil/But a good one shows well-ordering and coherence/. … And so under it, everything for mankind becomes whole and wise."[4]

—*Solon (c. 630–560 BCE), ancient Athenian statesman and a father of democracy*

"For if liberty and equality, as is thought by some, are chiefly to be found in democracy, they will be best attained when all persons alike share in the government to the utmost."[5]

—*Aristotle (384–322 BCE), ancient Athenian philosopher and teacher*

given absolute powers to fight terrorism?

Americans have had to consider questions like these since the September 11, 2001, attacks on the World Trade Center and on the Pentagon. Often in the past during wartime or rebellion, the U.S. government restricted civil liberties in order to make it easier to fight the enemy. These restrictions were lifted at the end of the unrest. The current war on terror, however, appears to have no visible end in sight. This uncertainty leaves many Americans wondering how long their rights are likely to be restricted in the name of keeping the country safe.

President George W. Bush at the site of the World Trade Center following the terrorist attacks of September 11, 2001

The Magna Carta

A Brief History of Civil Liberties: 1215–1789

As the attacks of September 11, 2001, clearly show, nations often face threats to their security from outside forces. In an effort to defend the country against harm, a government might reduce the civil rights of citizens, as the United States has done during times of war. Other times, the threat comes from within, as was the case with King John (1167–1216) of England. As a result of the situation he faced centuries ago, King John helped progress the idea of civil liberties.

King John's nobles had a challenge from their government that endangered their well-being and civil rights. The resolution the English nobles found would greatly influence the growth of civil rights in England and ultimately the United States.

King John was rich and educated and had a gift for politics. Still, not everything went well for him. The king lost all of the French lands that had been under his control. To make up for the loss of tax revenue from the French lands, King John raised the rents on his feudal lands and increased taxes. He also seized property when taxes were not paid and fined people for minor offenses. These actions made the king unpopular. He was even thrown out of the Catholic Church for refusing to accept the appointment of the archbishop by Pope Innocent.

King John eventually reconciled with the pope, but the split with the church left the king with a bad reputation among many English church officials. To make matters worse, the angry nobles rebelled against the king because they were upset over the increased taxes and other threats against their property and affairs. The rebels seized London, taking over England's most important city and the location of King John's government. The king was forced to make a deal with a council of 25 barons in order to continue his rule. In exchange for their demands, the rebels renewed their pledge of faithfulness to the king.

Civil Liberties and the Magna Carta

What did the nobles get in exchange for renewing their oaths? On June 15, 1215, King John signed the document that became known as the Magna Carta, which is Latin for "great charter." Some of the Magna Carta's 63 paragraphs concern civil liberties:

- "The English Church shall be free ... and its liberties unimpaired."[1]

- No one shall be arrested, imprisoned, or have his property seized without being judged by his peers or by the law of the land.

- Rights and justice will not be refused or delayed.

- Only judges, constables, sheriffs, and bailiffs who know the law and intend to observe it will be appointed.

- All unjust fines and unlawful property seizures shall be cancelled, and future fines will be decided by a council of 25 barons.

- The king, and anyone in the country who wishes, swear to obey the decisions of the 25 barons in all the above matters.

The council of barons eventually became England's Parliament. Initially, this group of nobles, which became known as the Great Council, served mainly to advise the king and to act as a court. By the fourteenth century, Parliament had grown into a large assembly that represented the upper class. From its original function as a court, Parliament eventually developed the power to consider petitions to correct complaints—later a key concept in the First Amendment. Parliament gradually gained the power to withhold financial support for the king until he accepted and acted on these petitions.

The Magna Carta

While it is unknown how many original copies of the Magna Carta were created, four exist today. The British Library has two copies. The other two copies are held in the cathedral archives in the cities of Lincoln and Salisbury in England.

PARLIAMENT'S GROWING POWER

Parliament's power fluctuated during the fifteenth and sixteenth centuries, depending on the forces and skill of the monarch in power. King James II (1633–1701) was Catholic in a predominantly Protestant England. When he tried to help his fellow Catholics, the king learned how difficult it was to rule without the support of Parliament. King James II tried to bypass Parliament by ordering all clergy to read a declaration in church that supported Catholics. The bishops refused. They were supported by William of Orange, King James II's son-in-law. Lacking popular support, King James II escaped to France. Parliament invited William to rule and invested him with power. This series of events became known as the Glorious Revolution of 1688. Parliament became supreme over the monarch by giving William the power to rule England. Parliament then passed the Bill of Rights of 1689, which proclaimed new civil rights that became the cornerstones of all future laws to preserve civil liberties.

British Parliament

In existence for more than 500 years, Parliament remains an important part of British government. British Parliament has three main roles:

- Examining and challenging the work of the government (scrutiny).
- Debating and passing all laws (legislation).
- Enabling the government to raise taxes.[2]

These liberties included the:

- Freedom to petition the king to correct an injustice without fear of punishment.

- Freedom of speech in Parliament (but not for the general population).

- Freedom from cruel and unusual punishment and excessive bail.

- Freedom from fines and forfeitures (government's taking of property) without trial.

The creation of protections for civil liberties had grown out of a disagreement between King James II and Parliament over which religion—Catholic or Protestant—should be the official one in England. Under the English Bill of Rights of 1689, the monarch had to swear to maintain the Protestant religion. Catholics were forbidden to serve as rulers of England.

Parliament would continue to represent only the nobility and wealthier classes until the Reform Bill of 1832 extended the vote. Parliament was more democratic and representative than it had been, but these characteristics were still limited. Only adult white men owning property—a limited portion of the population—could vote or take part in parliamentary activities.

AMERICA'S DECLARATION OF INDEPENDENCE

During the seventeenth century, while civil rights were developing in England, the English were also settling colonies in the New World. By the 1770s, the American colonies had thousands of new inhabitants and were busy and productive. However, the colonists were increasingly unhappy with British rule. In the colonies, a greater percentage of white adult men owned property than in England. Owning property entitled them to representation in Parliament. This fostered in them a strong sense of representational democracy and gave them high

George Mason and the Virginia Declaration of Rights

George Mason wrote and published the Virginia Declaration of Rights. Mason presented it to the Constitutional Convention June 12, 1776. The document influenced the Declaration of Independence. James Madison also drew on Mason's work when drafting the Bill of Rights in 1787. The Declaration of the Rights of Man and of the Citizen, a key document in the French Revolution of 1789, also shows the influence of Mason's work. In the Virginia Declaration of Rights, Mason wrote,

> That all men are by nature equally free and independent and have certain inherent rights ... namely, the enjoyment of life and liberty, with the means of ... pursuing and obtaining happiness.[3]

Mason's declaration was the first document to protect the rights of the individual rather than those of a particular group. Mason felt so strongly about the importance of these civil liberties that he was one of the few delegates to the Constitutional Convention who refused to sign the Constitution because it did not list these rights in the main part of the document.

expectations for their rulers. Their attitudes about government spread to their fellow colonists. The Americans realized what they were missing in government. In this way, a limited democracy in England spurred unrest in the colonies.

Initially, colonists' dissatisfaction with British rule was based primarily on economic factors—high taxes and lack of free trade. Colonists were also concerned about the lack of civil liberties. The British government was compromising the civil liberties that the colonists believed were their rights. For example, to crack down on smuggling, British officers in the colonies were allowed to search anyone's house or business without warning and take anything they thought had been smuggled.

In addition, American colonists were required to allow British soldiers to live in their homes. The British stifled political protest by accusing those who criticized the British government of seditious libel (making a false

Lee's Resolution to the Continental Congress

Richard Henry Lee was a representative of Virginia at the Continental Congress, the governing body of the thirteen colonies. On June 7, 1776, he brought forth the following resolution:

"Resolved, That these United Colonies are, and of right ought to be, free and independent States, that they are absolved from all allegiance to the British Crown, and that all political connection between them and the state of Great Britain is, and ought to be, totally dissolved."[4]

Benjamin Franklin, Thomas Jefferson, John Adams, Philip Livingston, and Roger Sherman work on the Declaration of Independence.

or damaging statement in writing). In a famous case of 1735, a New York printer, John Peter Zenger, was accused of libel for criticizing the New York colonial government in his newspaper, the *New York Weekly Journal.* Lawyer Andrew Hamilton successfully defended Zenger. The case established the principle that the government may not punish a publication for printing the truth about public matters.

As distrust grew between the American colonists and England, the British government made sure that judges who ruled in the colonies were chosen, paid, and controlled by the British rather than the Americans. Jury trials were often denied. Through the use of bills of attainder, in which citizens were declared corrupt, the British Parliament had the right to jail colonists, take away their property, and even execute them without a trial. In addition, any British officer accused of breaking the law overseas in the colonies would be tried in England rather than in the colony where the alleged crime took place.

Initially, the colonists considered themselves guarantors of English liberty. Few colonists wanted independence and fewer still expressed great political philosophy. Colonists' increasing frustration with the British government ultimately resulted in action. Just as the nobles under King John joined forces, colonist leaders united to separate America from England. The colonists created the Declaration of Independence to formally end these British practices in the United States.

Declaration of Independence on Display

The original Declaration of Independence still exists. Though it has faded, the document can be viewed in the Rotunda for the Charters of Freedom in the National Archives Building in Washington, D.C.

These issues were presented in the Declaration of Independence and addressed in the Constitution of the United States of America.

SACRIFICING FOR CIVIL LIBERTIES

The 56 men who signed the Declaration of Independence on July 4, 1776, strongly believed in the civil liberties they felt were being violated by the British. They knew that under British law their act of signing would be seen as treason, for which the penalty was death. These men took the laws of the colony seriously and were able to face the prospect of dying for a cause in which they believed. Together, the founding fathers fought for the colonists' independence from England. However, the men were not united in their belief about including a bill of rights in the Constitution nine years later. Had they changed their minds about the importance of these basic liberties?

United States of America

The term "United States of America" was used formally for the first time in the Declaration of Independence.

The Declaration of Independence

George Washington presides over the Constitutional Convention in 1787.

IS A BILL OF RIGHTS
NECESSARY?

*I*n 1787, four years after winning the United
States's independence from England, the
founding fathers met in Philadelphia to draft a
constitution. The document did not originally
include a bill of rights. Initially, the framers of the

Constitution were more focused on creating a strong federal government than on protecting individual rights. For the previous six years, the new nation had been governed by the Articles of Confederation, a document that was weak in its power over the states. It did not provide for a president, had no power to tax in order to pay for services, and had no way to enforce laws except through the individual states. The result was a weak central government that was almost bankrupt.

To correct these problems, the framers created a seven-section document that laid out the powers of the government. The first three sections were the most important. They defined three branches of government: legislative, executive, and judicial. They also spelled out a system of checks and balances to ensure that no one branch was stronger than the others. For example, the executive branch, or president, could veto a bill passed by Congress, but Congress could override that veto with a two-thirds vote of its members.

Articles of Confederation

The United States' first constitution was the Articles of Confederation. The Continental Congress, the first national government of the United States, approved the Articles of Confederation November 15, 1777. In order for the document to be accepted nationwide, all 13 states had to ratify it. This did not happen until March 1, 1781. The Articles were replaced by the U.S. Constitution March 4, 1789.

With these guidelines for a strong federal government in place, the framers turned their attention to the rights of individual citizens. There was much debate over whether individual freedoms should be detailed in the Constitution.

The Constitution Was Different

In the discussions of what the Constitution should embody, several speakers argued against including a bill of rights. Looking back at England's Magna Carta and the Bill of Rights of 1689, Alexander Hamilton noted that these were agreements "between kings and their subjects."[1] Hamilton argued that the Constitution was different from these documents. The most important difference is suggested by the Constitution's first three words, "We the people." The Constitution was an agreement among the people themselves, not between rulers and those ruled. Since "the people" would not logically want to reduce their own rights by listing only those rights that should be protected, a separate bill of rights was

"All the powers, which the bill of rights guard against the abuse of, are contained or implied in the general ones granted by this constitution."[2]

—Robert Yates, Anti-Federalist and judge writing under the name of Brutus (the Roman senator who assassinated Julius Caesar to prevent him from getting too much power in ancient Rome)

Alexander Hamilton, a Federalist, opposed adding a bill of rights to the U.S. Constitution.

not necessary. The Constitution and the Bill of Rights were essentially the same thing in Hamilton's view.

Hamilton also noted that a bill of rights might be dangerous. Such a bill might encourage lawmakers to

George Mason, an Anti-Federalist, was in favor of adding a bill of rights to the U.S. Constitution.

claim more powers for the people than were warranted, which would weaken the balance of the central government. Hamilton was a leading figure in a group of delegates that became known as the Federalists. The Federalists believed a strong central government would be more effective in passing, enforcing, and interpreting laws.

PROTECTION AGAINST ANOTHER MONARCHY

The Anti-Federalists—those in favor of stronger rights for states—argued that if the government was too strong and did not protect individual rights, it could become like the monarchy in Great Britain. In the words of George Mason, if the Constitution was passed without such a bill,

> *The Congress may grant monopolies in trade and commerce, [create] new crimes, inflict unusual and severe punishments, and extend their power as far as they shall think proper; so that the State legislatures have no security for the powers now presumed to remain to them; or the people for their rights.*[3]

Fellow Anti-Federalists who supported Mason's views included Patrick Henry, John Adams, John Hancock, and Thomas Jefferson. Jefferson noted that a bill of rights in the Constitution would give the Supreme Court the power to limit those who would try to restrict basic freedoms. Jefferson wrote to James Madison about his fear of an unchecked Congress, stating,

I have a right to nothing which another has the right to take away. … A bill of rights is what the people are entitled to against every government on earth, general or particular; and what no just government should refuse, or rest on inferences.[4]

A Compromise on the Bill of Rights

The debate over a bill of rights was impassioned. To make sure their discussions were completely private, all the doors and windows in the room where the delegates met were kept closed.

A compromise was finally reached. Jefferson and Adams persuaded Madison,

Madison's Change of Mind

One of the major writers of the Constitution and creator of the three-branch system, James Madison began his political career as a Federalist. He thought a bill of rights was unnecessary because of the way the Constitution divided power among the three branches of government. Through a system of checks and balances, the Constitution would ensure that no one branch was dominant. In Madison's mind, the executive branch under this system was not likely to produce a tyrant who would take away citizens' civil liberties.

Madison's change of mind was influenced by multiple forces. First, Thomas Jefferson and John Adams, both of whom Madison greatly respected, had declared themselves in favor of a bill of rights that would safeguard citizens' freedoms. Second, Madison realized that his own political future might be in danger if he continued to support the Federalist cause. Third, Madison also realized that backing the addition of a bill of rights meant that the Anti-Federalists would ratify the Constitution—the most important issue at the time. With Madison's change of opinion, the Anti-Federalists now agreed to support the Constitution. The drive toward ratification had taken a step forward. Madison then became a leader in the drafting of the proposed Bill of Rights.

who had been considered a Federalist,
to swing his support to the Anti-
Federalists. The Anti-Federalists
agreed to approve the new
Constitution without a bill of rights as
long as one would be added later.

THE BILL OF RIGHTS BECOMES PART OF THE CONSTITUTION

By the summer of 1789, two
years after the Constitution had
been drafted at the Philadelphia
Convention, 11 states had approved
the document—two more than the
required nine needed to ratify.
Meeting in New York, Congress now
took on the task of crafting a bill of
rights. Madison took a lead role in

Debating the Bill of Rights

In the debate over the proposed Bill of Rights, Federalist delegate Theodore Sedgwick asked mockingly why these bills did not specify that "a man should have the right to wear his hat if he pleased; that he might get up when he pleased, and go to bed when he thought proper."[5] Replying in a more serious tone, an Anti-Federalist congressman reminded the delegates that monarchs in the past had routinely required that their subjects remove their hats.

drafting a proposal. Despite the bitterness of previous
debates on the issue, the House of Representatives and
Senate reached a consensus. They promptly passed a list
of a dozen proposed amendments that were sent to the
states for ratification. The first two amendments
concerned congressional appointments and pay. These
were rejected. The other ten became part of the U.S.

French Declaration of the Rights of Man and the Citizen

The French Declaration of the Rights of Man and of the Citizen (1789) was greatly influenced by the U.S. Bill of Rights. Echoing that section of the U.S. Constitution, the French Declaration states, "The free communication of ideas and opinions is one of the most precious of the rights of man. Any citizen may, therefore, speak, write, and publish freely."[6]

Constitution on December 15, 1791, when Virginia became the eleventh state to approve them.

In a turn of events that surprised many, the Bill of Rights would soon be challenged during the presidency of a man who had been one of its strongest supporters: John Adams.

Done in Convention, by the unanimous confent of the States prefent, the feventeenth day of September, in the year of our Lord one thoufand feven hundred and eighty-feven, and of the Independence of the United States of America the twelfth. In witnefs whereof we have hereunto fubfcribed our Names.

GEORGE WASHINGTON, Prefident,
And Deputy from VIRGINIA.

NEW-HAMPSHIRE.	{ John Langdon, Nicholas Gilman.		George Read, Gunning Bedford, Junior,
MASSACHUSETTS.	{ Nathaniel Gorham, Rufus King.	DELAWARE.	{ John Dickinfon, Richard Baffett, Jacob Broom.
CONNECTICUT	{ William Samuel Johnfon, Roger Sherman.		{ James M·Henry,
NEW-YORK.	Alexander Hamilton.	MARYLAND.	{ Daniel of St. Tho Jenifer, Daniel Carrol.
NEW-JERSEY.	{ William Livingfton, David Brearley, William Paterfon, Jonathan Dayton.	VIRGINIA.	{ John Blair, James Madifon, Junior.
PENNSYLVANIA.	{ Benjamin Franklin, Thomas Mifflin, Robert Morris, George Clymer, Thomas Fitzfimons, Jared Ingerfoll, James Wilfon, Gouverneur Morris.	NORTH-CAROLINA	{ William Blount, Richard Dobbs Spaight, Hugh Williamson.
		SOUTH-CAROLINA.	{ John Rutledge, Charles CoteswortbPinckney Charles Pinckney. Pierce Butler.
		GEORGIA.	{ William Few, Abraham Baldwin.

Atteft, William *Jackson*, SECRETARY.

IN CONVENTION, Monday September 17th, 1787.
PRESENT
The States of New-Hampfhire, Maffachufetts, Connecticut, Mr. *Hamilton* from New-York, New-Jerfey, Pennfylvania, Delaware, Maryland, Virginia, North-Carolina, South-Carolina and Georgia:

RESOLVED,

THAT the preceding *Conftitution be laid before the United States in Congrefs affembled, and that it is the opinion of this Convention, that it fhould afterwards be fubmitted to a Convention of Delegates, chofen in each State by the People thereof, under the recommendation of its Legiflature, for their affent and ratification; and that each Convention affenting to, and ratifying the fame, fhould give Notice thereof, to the United States in Congrefs affembled.*

Refolved, *That it is the opinion of this Convention, that as foon as the Conventions of nine States fhall have ratified this Conftitution, the United States in Congrefs affembled fhould fix a day on which Electors fhould be appointed by the States which fhall have ratified the fame, and a day on which the Electors fhould affemble to vote for the Prefident, and the time and place for commencing proceedings under this Conftitution. That after fuch publication the Electors fhould be appointed, and the Senators and Reprefentatives elected: That the Electors fhould meet on the day fixed for the Election of the Prefident, and fhould tranfmit their votes certified, figned, fealed and directed, as the Conftitution requires, to the Secretary of the United States in Congrefs affembled, that the Senators and Reprefentatives fhould convene at the time and place affigned; that the Senators fhould appoint a Prefident of the Senate, for the fole purpofe of receiving, opening and counting the votes for Prefident; and, that after he fhall be chofen, the Congrefs, together with the Prefident, fhould, without delay, proceed to execute this Conftitution.*

By the unanimous Order of the Convention,
GEORGE WASHINGTON, Prefident.

William Jackson, Secretary

Resolution to ratify the U.S. Constitution, dated September 17, 1787

John Adams was the first U.S. president to limit civil liberties.

LIMITING CIVIL LIBERTIES
FOR NATIONAL SECURITY

he situation faced by President John Adams
in 1798 was similar to the one President
George W. Bush would face after the events of
September 11, 2001. The federal government was
threatened by terrorist attacks, rumors abounded about

foreign plots to destroy the capital and harm American citizens, and anti-immigrant feelings were growing.

After its king was overthrown in 1789, France was ruled by mobs of people. The success of the French people in overthrowing their monarchy encouraged other citizens in Europe to revolt against their leaders. There were rumors that France might invade the United States and that the more than 20,000 French immigrants then living in the United States would assist. President Adams's own nephew blamed all of the country's problems on the immigrants living in the United States. He argued that the United States should stop being a refuge for foreigners.

Since becoming a country, war, or the threat of war, has often threatened civil liberties in the United States. John Adams was the first U.S. president to set the pattern of reducing civil liberties when threatened by unrest, whether the threat was at home or abroad.

John Adams and Fear of the French

In an atmosphere of fear, Adams signed four laws known as the Alien and Sedition Acts of 1798:

- The Alien Enemies Act permitted the U.S. government to deport noncitizens who came from any nation with which the United States was at war.

- The Alien Friends Act allowed the president, during peacetime, to deport any alien he thought to be dangerous.

- The Naturalization Act extended the period that an immigrant must live in the United States before becoming a citizen from 5 years to 14 years.

- The Sedition Act prohibited speaking or writing "false, scandalous and malicious writing or writings against the government of the United States."[1]

Supported by the Federalists in Congress, Adams's action was an attempt to control what he saw as threats to the very existence of the young nation. However, the Sedition Act was widely viewed as a Federalist attempt to silence its political opponents. Ten people, mostly journalists, were convicted under the act.

In the early 1800s, the government and laws changed. In 1800, the Alien Friends Act expired, and Adams lost his bid for reelection to his opponent, Thomas Jefferson. By 1802, the Federalists were defeated in Congress as well, largely because of the unpopularity of the Alien and Sedition Acts of 1798. The Federalists now occupied only 39 of 142 seats in Congress, making them the minority party. Even with these changes, a model had been established to restrict

First Amendment rights during war or domestic states of unrest—a model that has been followed for two centuries. By the mid-1800s, circumstances would present another president with the challenge of whether to limit civil liberties. Abraham Lincoln did just that during the Civil War.

Restricted Legal Rights during the Civil War

During the Civil War, President Lincoln jailed many civilians without a hearing before a judge. Latin for "you shall have the body," habeas corpus is one of the oldest concepts in English common law. It means that individuals who are arrested must be brought before a judge and charged with a crime before being put on trial. Article I, Section 9 of the Constitution permits suspension of habeas corpus only when "in cases of rebellion or invasion the public safety may require it."[2] Lincoln's order to suspend habeas corpus was intended to apply to Confederate spies, draft resisters, and anyone who showed disloyalty to the Union. Lincoln's decision was later found to be illegal in *Ex Parte Milligan.*

Lamdin P. Milligan, an American citizen and resident of Indiana, and four others had been caught planning to steal Union weapons and use them to free Confederate prisoners in Union prisons. Milligan and his group were tried, convicted, and sentenced to hang by a military court. Milligan appealed the conviction on the basis of unlawful imprisonment. In 1866, the Supreme Court ruled 9–0 that suspension of habeas corpus was unconstitutional, even during wartime, in a state where civilian courts were still operating. Military courts could try civilians only in states where civil courts had been closed. Milligan and the others had been caught and tried in Indiana, a state in which civil courts operated during the Civil War.

In Favor: National Safety over Individual Rights

Should habeas corpus be suspended during wartime? Supporters of this policy say the nation's political survival is more important than an individual's rights, especially someone who may be aiding the enemy. Lincoln said military courts were better suited than civilian courts to handle the number of cases that occur during a civil war. He also claimed those being arrested endangered public safety, and needed to be locked up.

Military tribunals differ from civilian courts in many ways. In

"The sacred rights of mankind are not to be rummaged for, among old parchments, or musty records. They are written, as with a sun beam in the whole volume of human nature, by the hand of the divinity itself; and can never be erased or obscured by mortal power."[3]

—Alexander Hamilton

military courts, the accused are usually
enemy soldiers who are charged,
prosecuted, judged, and sentenced by
military officers. Rules of evidence are
less strict in a military court than in a
civilian court, and trials are often
secret. Conviction is by majority rather
than unanimous vote, and there are no
appeals.

"Liberty lies in the hearts of
men and women; when it
dies there, no constitution,
no law, no court can even
do much to help it. While
it lies there it needs no
constitution, no law, no
court to save it."[4]

—*Federal Judge Learned
Hand (1872–1961)*

The advantage of military tribunals is
that they provide swift justice. As with civil trials, a
military tribunal ensures that the defendant is
informed of the charges, represented by a lawyer, and
allowed to present a defense. More recently, under the
Military Commissions Act of 2006, the defendant is
given the right to appeal the verdict of a military
tribunal to a civilian court.

Opposed: Democracy Must Be Maintained

Opponents of Lincoln's decision pointed out that if
a democracy at war still wants to call itself democratic, it
must maintain the basic civil rights in which it believes.
Otherwise, the country risks becoming the very thing it
claims to be against—a dictatorship that does not
recognize civil liberties. In 1862, Supreme Court

Chief Justice Roger Taney declared Lincoln's act unconstitutional. Taney declared that suspension of habeas corpus required an act of Congress. However, Lincoln refused to obey the ruling.

Lincoln's limitation of habeas corpus during the Civil War was not the last time a U.S. president restricted civil rights. Woodrow Wilson did so as well 50 years later.

LIMITED CIVIL LIBERTIES DURING WORLD WAR I

To discourage anti-war feelings in the United States during World War I, President Woodrow Wilson supported two laws that limited civil liberties:

- The Espionage Act of 1917 made it a crime to pass information meant to "interfere with the operation or success of the military or naval forces of the United States to promote the success of its enemies."[5]

- The Sedition Act of 1918 forbade "scurrilous [offensive] or abusive language" about the U.S. government, flag, or armed forces.[6]

Under the Sedition Act, Charles Schenck, a Socialist, was convicted of giving pamphlets attacking the draft (a system of selecting people to serve in the

President Woodrow Wilson limited civil liberties during World War I with the Espionage Act of 1917 and the Sedition Act of 1918.

military) to young men of draft age. The U.S. Supreme Court unanimously upheld the conviction. In the landmark opinion *Schenck v. United States,* Chief Justice Holmes wrote a famous decision that is still quoted today: "The most stringent protection of free speech would not protect a man in falsely shouting fire in a theater and causing a panic." For Holmes, protection of speech by the First Amendment was not justified if the words used created a "clear and present danger that they will bring about the substantive evils that Congress has a right to protect."[7]

The Espionage Act of 1917 and the Sedition Act of 1918 were upheld with this ruling. The executive branch's limitation of civil liberties during times of war went even further during the next world war.

Eugene V. Debs

In 1918, Eugene V. Debs, a Socialist union organizer and activist, gave an antiwar speech in Canton, Ohio. Most of his speech described how wars are always declared by the rich but fought by the poor. Debs praised antiwar socialists of the past, urged his listeners to oppose the current war (World War I), and asked them to organize other workers. Debs commended current antiwar activists who were serving jail terms for opposing the draft, saying, "I am proud of them; they are there for us; and we are here for them."[8]

As a result of the speech, Debs was arrested, convicted under the Sedition Act of 1918, and sentenced to ten years in jail. He appealed to the Supreme Court and lost. Justice Holmes noted how similar *Debs v. United States* was to the earlier case *Schenck v. United States*. While in prison, Debs ran for president on the Socialist ticket. He received almost one million votes. Debs served more than two years of his sentence before President Harding pardoned him in 1921. Debs died five years later at the age of 70.

JAPANESE–AMERICAN DETENTION DURING WORLD WAR II

After the Japanese attack of Pearl Harbor in 1941, President Franklin Delano Roosevelt signed Executive Order 9066 in 1942. The order authorized the detention of more than 110,000 Japanese-Americans living along the West Coast of the United States. Families were forced to leave their homes and move inland. The detainees were housed in rough barracks surrounded by barbed wire and watched by armed guards. These Japanese-Americans were isolated from the rest of the United States for four years. By this time, most of the detainees' homes and property had been damaged, stolen, or destroyed. Many were left with nothing.

In Favor: Better Safe Than Sorry

Were these detention camps justified in any way? Milton Eisenhower was head of the War Relocation Authority, the government agency in charge of relocating Japanese-Americans to detention camps. He defended the detention, explaining that many of the Japanese-Americans lived near shipyards, oil wells, naval bases, and other vital wartime resources, and "no one knew what would happen among this concentrated population if Japanese forces should try to invade our shores."[9]

Fred Korematsu was one Japanese-American who refused to leave his home. He sued the United States, and his case was eventually reviewed in the Supreme Court. He lost the case in a 6–3 vote in which the majority of justices ruled as follows:

The Jerome Relocation Center near Jerome, Arkansas, was home to thousands of Japanese-Americans from California during World War II.

When under conditions of modern warfare our shores are threatened by hostile forces, the power to protect must be commensurate with the threatened danger. ... There was evidence of disloyalty on the part of some, the military authorities considered that the need for action was great, and time was short. We cannot—by availing ourselves of the calm perspectives of hindsight—now say that at that time these actions were unjustified.[10]

Opposed: Executive Order 9066 Is Racist

The three justices in the minority on *Korematsu v. United States* (1944) ruled that Executive Order 9066 was racist because it targeted an entire ethnic group instead of specific individuals. These judges charged that the majority justified a military decision on the mistaken assumption that all Japanese-Americans tend to be pro-Japanese. In fact, almost 75 percent of the detainees were American citizens, and many had relatives serving in the American armed forces.

After the Crisis Ends

What happens to civil liberties after wartime? Those in favor of laws that restrict individual freedoms argue that similar laws in the past have not permanently damaged civil liberties. Such laws are meant to cover only the crisis at hand, not future crises. For example, after World War I ended, the Sedition Act of 1918 was overturned.

Others reply that many such laws stay active for years. For example, large parts of the Espionage Act remain part of U.S. law today, decades after World

Korematsu Ruling Overturned

The 1944 ruling against Fred Korematsu for evading detention was overturned in 1983, though the detention itself was never ruled illegal. Nevertheless, the U.S. government later apologized to Japanese-Americans for their reloca-tion and paid over $1.2 billion in reparations and $400 million in benefits to the victims. This amounted to about $20,000 per person.

War I ended. These critics argue that such laws unfairly punish those who are only expressing unpopular opinions.

THE WAR ON TERROR

The attacks of September 11, 2001, marked a new chapter in the balance between national security and the maintenance of civil liberties. For President Bush, they justified new executive powers in the treatment of enemy prisoners and the definition of *enemy*. He claimed the right to imprison anyone who met his definition—even American citizens. Acting swiftly after the attacks, Congress passed the USA Patriot Act in October 2001, which gave the president expanded powers intended to allow the president to act faster during crisis to defend against further attacks. Despite strong support in Congress for the law, at least 408 communities and five states later passed measures opposing the Patriot Act for specific violations of the Bill of Rights.

"The Department of Justice's first priority is to prevent future terrorist attacks. Since its passage following the September 11, 2001 attacks, the Patriot Act has played a key part—and often the leading role—in a number of successful operations to protect innocent Americans from the deadly plans of terrorists dedicated to destroying America and our way of life. While the results have been important, in passing the Patriot Act, Congress provided for only modest, incremental changes in the law. Congress simply took existing legal principles and retrofitted them to preserve the lives and liberty of the American people from the challenges posed by a global terrorist network."[11]

—*U.S. Department of Justice*

This list of wanted persons deemed "Dangerous religious terrorists" by the Pakistan government are members of al-Qaeda, including Osama bin Laden, pictured top left, mastermind of the attacks of September 11, 2001.

A young man learns about the First Amendment at the
McCormick Tribune Freedom Museum in Chicago, Illinois.

THE FIRST AMENDMENT

*M*ost Americans are aware of their right
to free speech. Because it prohibits the
government's limiting of speech, the First Amendment
may be the most important part of the Constitution.
Without the freedom to speak their minds, the framers

could not have written the Constitution. The many difficult issues facing them could only be resolved if the framers agreed to respect each other's right to hold different opinions and to speak freely.

Speech is one of several freedoms the First Amendment protects. It also guarantees freedom of the press, freedom of religion, freedom to assemble, and freedom to address the government. Freedom of the press and freedom of religion are two rights that have been challenged since the attacks of September 11.

FREEDOM OF THE PRESS: ACCESS TO TRIALS

After September 11, the U.S. government closed to the public and the press all deportation hearings (trials to determine whether to send a noncitizen back to his or her country) that might have some connection to terrorism. However, the government has never given a reason for this policy. As an extension of the First Amendment, trials historically have been open to both the press and the public. This freedom was tested in 2002 in the case of Rabih Haddad. He operated an Islamic charity suspected of

"Congress shall make no law respecting an establishment of religion, or prohibiting the free exercise thereof; or abridging the freedom of speech, or of the press; or the right of the people peaceably to assemble, and to petition the Government for a redress of grievances."[1]

—*Amendment I*
U.S. Constitution

supplying funds to terrorist organizations. The *Detroit Free Press* was denied access to Haddad's deportation hearing. The newspaper and the American Civil Liberties Union (ACLU) sued the federal government and won in both the federal district and appeals court. The U.S. District Court judge, Nancy Edmund, cited the First Amendment, ruling that the rights of the individual were more important than the government's need for secrecy and allowed the hearings to be open to the public and media. Judge Edmund said,

> It is important for the public, particularly individuals who feel that they are being targeted by the government as a result of the terrorist attacks of September 11, to know that even during these sensitive times the government is adhering to immigration procedures and respecting individuals' rights. Openness is necessary for the public to maintain confidence in the value and soundness of the government's actions, as secrecy only breeds suspicion as to why the government is proceeding against Haddad and aliens like him.[2]

"The basis of our government being the opinion of the people, the very first object should be to keep that right; and were it left to me to decide whether we should have a government without newspapers or newspapers without a government, I should not hesitate a moment to prefer the latter."[3]

— *Thomas Jefferson*

In a similar case in New Jersey, however, a U.S. Court of Appeals judge ruled that the history of

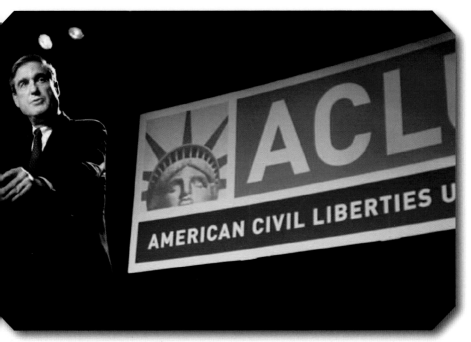

FBI Director Robert Mueller addresses the American Civil Liberties Union 2003 Inaugural Membership Conference on June 13, 2003, in Washington, D.C.

opening deportation hearings to the public was not strong enough to balance the possibly negative effects on national security. The defeated plaintiffs asked the U.S. Supreme Court to review the case, but the request was declined.

In these cases, the issue was whether the government's interest in national security was more important than public access to trials. Without rationale for the government's decision, citizens are left to guess why the deportation hearings were closed and what exactly is happening during the trials. For some Americans, limiting access to trials increases doubt about or distrust in the government. This is because citizens' rights are being limited and the government's actions behind the closed doors of the trials are unknown. The government cannot be held accountable for actions of which its citizens are unaware.

Is There Freedom of Speech in School?

Three key cases involving student expression deal with the issue of freedom of speech in school.

In 1969, 12 students were sent home for wearing black armbands to protest the Vietnam War. They sued the local school board and won. In *Tinker v. Des Moines*, the Supreme Court ruled:

> A prohibition against expression of opinion, without any evidence that the rule is necessary to avoid substantial interference with school discipline or the rights of others, is not permissible under the First and Fourteenth Amendments.[4]

In 1986, a student was suspended for two days for using what some believed was inappropriate language in a speech to students. He sued. The Supreme Court ruled in *Bethel School District v. Fraser* that the speech was not protected by the First Amendment because such language was inconsistent with the educational values.

In 1988, the Court upheld the right of school officials to censor stories about teen pregnancy and divorce from a school newspaper. In *Hazelwood School District v. Kuhlmeier,* the Court ruled that there had been no First Amendment violation— the rights of public school students are not automatically the same as those of adults outside school because a school has a basic educational mission. The school newspaper is essentially an educational class and not a place for public, personal expression.

Freedom of Religion:
Being Muslim post-September 11

When President Bush addressed Congress and the nation shortly after September 11, he declared war on al-Qaeda, not upon Islam. He stated that Islam's "teachings are good and peaceful, and those who commit evil in the name of Allah blaspheme the name of Allah."[5] Even with President Bush's statement, since September 11, Muslims have been discriminated against on the basis of their faith. This is particularly so in U.S. military prisons at Guantanamo Bay, Cuba, and in Afghanistan. *Newsweek* magazine rescinded one story involving alleged disrespect by prison guards for the Koran, but there have been numerous similar claims. For example, on Russian television in June 2004, Aryat Vahitov, a former Guantanamo detainee, said that U.S. prison officials "tore the Koran to pieces in front of us, threw it into the toilet."[6] Such an act does not fit the founding fathers' idea that people should be able to worship and practice their religion without fear of attack. But do such rules apply in times of crisis when known attackers are of a certain religion?

Islam

With more than one billion followers, Islam is the second largest religion in the world. Practicers of Islam are called Muslims. Muslims believe in one god, Allah. The Islamic holy book is the Koran, or Qur'an.

A Delicate Balance

Balancing personal civil liberties with other governmental concerns is a formidable task. This difficulty, while felt especially during wartime, also presents a continuing challenge during peacetime. The nation's opinions and values gradually change over time, as does the makeup of the Supreme Court, which may express these values in its decisions.

Challenges to the First Amendment, while important, have not been the only challenge to the Bill of Rights in the post-September 11 era. Most cases have challenged the Fourth Amendment's guarantee against unreasonable searches and seizures. Privacy has been a major issue. Continual reports in the media note that the government is using technology to randomly listen to citizens' telephone conversations and to read their personal e-mails.

A section of a ninth-century Koran, the holy book of Islam, written in gold leaf

A statue of George Washington stands out above protesters holding up signs critical of the USA Patriot Act during a demonstration near the New York Stock Exchange.

THE FOURTH AMENDMENT

he word *privacy* does not appear in the U.S. Constitution. Yet the idea is addressed in the Fourth Amendment's "right of the people to be secure … against unreasonable searches and seizures."[1] The question is: What action amounts to a search?

Obviously, this freedom applies to a person's house. The Supreme Court has ruled that the area immediately surrounding one's home is also off limits. But suppose a person owns a lot of land. In that case, the Court has ruled that any land not visible from a public road does not require a government permit to search, even if "No Trespassing" signs are posted. Similarly, a police helicopter may legally observe property from 400 feet (192 m) above the ground without invading the owner's privacy.

THE RIGHT TO BE SECURE AGAINST UNREASONABLE SEARCHES AND SEIZURES

Without a court warrant, does the government have the right to track private communications? After September 11, President Bush secretly approved a program to monitor, without court approval, thousands of telephone conversations and e-mail messages between people abroad and people in the United States. The program continued until January 2007.

"The right of the people to be secure in their persons, houses, papers, and effects, against unreasonable searches and seizures, shall not be violated, and no Warrants shall issue, but upon probable cause, supported by Oath or affirmation, and particularly describing the place to be searched, and the persons or things to be seized."[2]

—*Amendment IV*
U.S. Constitution

On December 20, 2006, the president signed a postal reform measure. Similar to previous laws, the new law requires a search warrant to open first-class mail unless postal inspectors think it contains a dangerous substance. President Bush, however, added a signing statement to the measure in which he announced that he would interpret it "in a manner consistent ... with the need to conduct searches in exigent [critical] circumstances."[3] In other words, President Bush gave postal authorities much greater leeway to use their judgment in interpreting the law. He has always emphasized that the president needs the power to act with speed and agility in order to combat terrorist threats that are by their very nature intended to be carried out swiftly and without warning. Expanding postal authorities' power helps the president meet that need.

In addition to criticizing the telephone and e-mail monitoring program and the postal reform measure, civil liberties organizations have questioned three sections of the 2001 USA Patriot Act: Section 215, Section 805, and Section 505. The organizations claim that these sections may violate the Fourth Amendment. For example, the government now has the right to spy on a citizen simply because he or she wrote a negative letter about the government or the president to the editor of a newspaper.

USA PATRIOT ACT: SECTION 215

Section 215 of the USA Patriot Act is the first section in dispute. According to this section, the FBI may demand records and personal belongings of individuals. Partly in response to concerns about civil liberties, Congress revised this section of the act in 2006. Under the revision, those who are required to provide information have the right to consult a lawyer. Also, each government request must include a statement that there are "reasonable grounds" for demanding the items. The individuals are still subject to a gag order that forbids them to tell anyone other than their lawyers that they received a demand for records. Individuals may challenge the demand in court, but judges are expected to respect the government's view that secrecy is necessary.

Reasonable and Unreasonable Searches

At the airport departure gate, travelers submit to having their bodies traced with a wand that detects metallic objects. Few travelers object because they recognize that the search is a reasonable way of helping to ensure safe flights. However, suppose a car is stopped and the driver is given a ticket for speeding. The police are not allowed by law to search the car because it makes no sense to assume that such a search would reveal more evidence of speeding. Only if a person is arrested for a crime after the car is stopped may the police legally search the vehicle and the driver. The reason for the search is to make sure the person is not carrying a concealed weapon or hiding evidence of a crime.

USA Patriot Act: Section 805

Under the second disputed section of the Patriot

Government Access of Library Records

In Favor: Heather Mac Donald argues that the Fourth Amendment right to privacy is not relevant when it comes to library patrons:

> By publicly borrowing library books, patrons forfeit any constitutional protections they may have had in their reading habits. ... Grand juries investigating a crime have always been able to subpoena the very items covered by [Section] 215 [of the Patriot Act]—including library records and Internet logs—without seeking a warrant or indeed any judicial approval at all. Section 215 merely gives anti-terror investigators the same access to records as criminal grand juries, with the added protection of judicial oversight.[4]

Opposed: The ACLU argues against the government accessing library records:

> Section 215 violates the Fourth Amendment because it authorizes the FBI to conduct intrusive investigations without probable cause and without notice. ... Section 215 also violates the First Amendment because it chills free speech and unjustifiably prevents organizations from disclosing even to innocent people that their privacy has been compromised.[5]

Congress has since revised Section 215 to allow targets of such investigations to disclose their status to a lawyer and require that the FBI show reasonable grounds "to believe that the tangible things sought are 'relevant' to an authorized or preliminary investigation."[6]

Act, Section 805 (a)(2)(b), it is illegal to provide "material support or resources," including "expert assistance or advice," to terrorist organizations. Several groups have sued the government, claiming that the ban on expert advice and assistance is so vague that it could bar activities protected by the First Amendment. For example, helping a group in petitioning the United Nations,

advising on international law, and
assisting in negotiating peace
agreements could all be considered
"expert assistance or advice."

USA Patriot Act: Section 505

The third controversial section,
Section 505, expands the FBI's
authority to issue National Security
Letters (NSLs). NSLs require citizens
to produce, without court approval,
records from organizations,
including libraries. According to a
report in the *Washington Post,* the FBI
issues more than 30,000 NSLs a year. Once limited to
the records of suspected terrorists or foreign spies, the
FBI can now seek information about anyone. Further,
as in Section 215, Section 505 puts recipients of an
NSL under a gag order that prohibits them from telling
anyone about it. In *Doe v. Gonzalez* (2005), Connecticut
librarians successfully challenged a gag order on an
NSL that demanded library patron records. In June
2006, the FBI withdrew the NSL. As of December
2006, several suits are proceeding that question the
legality of Section 505.

**American Civil
Liberties Union**

The American Civil Liberties Union (ACLU) was
founded in 1920 by a few
civil liberties activists.
Today, the organization
boasts more than 500,000
members and supporters,
with offices in every state.
Through its offices, the
ACLU handles thousands
of court cases every year.
The ACLU's mission is to
uphold the rights set forth
in the Bill of Rights and
other amendments for all
people in the United States.

"The greatest dangers to liberty lurk in insidious encroachment [a slow takeover] by men of zeal, well-meaning but without understanding."[7]

—U.S. Supreme Court Justice Louis Brandeis in Olmstead v. United States, a wiretapping case

These cases all illustrate the need to balance constitutional rights to privacy with legitimate efforts to combat terrorist forces. Denying the president the power he needs to fight terrorism could provide unintended support for the very forces the president is trying to fight. On the other hand, unquestioning support of the executive branch may lead to the loss of the rights for which the country is fighting.

During a news conference, FBI Director Robert Mueller discusses the gathering of personal information.

Camp Delta is a U.S. detention center in Guantanamo Bay, Cuba.

Habeas Corpus and
Due Process

abeas corpus is one of the oldest and most important concepts in law. It ensures that a person who has been arrested will be brought before a judge and officially charged with a crime. Habeas corpus is one of the key ideas in the larger concept of due process. Anyone charged with a crime will go through due process, an accepted set of correct and proper procedures. Habeas corpus is addressed in Article I of the Constitution. Due process is detailed in the Fifth Amendment. The Constitution stresses that these rights may be put on hold only in times of extreme danger.

Until recently, Lincoln's suspension of habeas corpus during the Civil War was the only time in U.S. history that right was restricted. However, both habeas corpus and due process have been limited during the United States's war on terror.

Suspension of Habeas Corpus and Due Process

During the U.S. invasion of Afghanistan in 2001, American forces captured an American citizen named Yaser Hamdi. The government classified Hamdi as an "enemy combatant" and held him for more than two years at various military brigs, or jails.

"The privilege of the Writ [court order] of Habeas Corpus shall not be suspended, unless when in Cases of Rebellion or Invasion the public Safety may require it."[1]

—*Article 1, Section 9 U.S. Constitution*

"No person shall be held to answer for a … crime, unless on … indictment of a Grand Jury, except in cases arising in the land or naval forces … when in actual service in time of War or public danger; nor shall any person … be deprived of life, liberty, or property, without due process of law."[2]

—*Amendment V U.S. Constitution*

During this time, Hamdi was neither charged with a crime nor given access to a lawyer.

PROTECTING AGAINST ENEMY COMBATANTS

Was Hamdi's capture justified? According to President Bush, it was, since Hamdi was classified as an "enemy combatant." There are two types of enemy combatants. Lawful combatants are granted prisoner-of-war (POW) status. Unlawful combatants are not. Al-Qaeda members are deemed unlawful combatants because they do not fit the criteria set forth by the Geneva Convention. There are multiple Geneva Conventions. The Third Geneva

---

Ex Parte Quirin and Enemy Combatant

The concept of an "unlawful enemy combatant" came in part from *Ex Parte Quirin,* a Supreme Court decision from the World War II era. Eight German spies (one of whom was a U.S. citizen) landed by submarine on the East Coast with orders to destroy the United States' war industries. The men were caught, tried by a secret military tribunal, convicted, and sentenced to death. The ruling described an unlawful combatant as one "who without uniform comes secretly through the lines for the purpose of waging war by destruction of life or property, are familiar examples of belligerents who are generally deemed not to be entitled to the status of prisoners of war, but to be offenders against the law of war subject to trial and punishment by military tribunals."[3]

Seven years later, however, Geneva Convention Article IV mentioned no such kind of combatant in the section describing prisoners of war. Instead, it referred broadly to several categories. These included members of armed forces, members of militias or volunteer corps, and civilians and noncombatants who happened to be in the battlefield area and were detained.

Convention, the Geneva Convention Relative to the Treatment of Prisoners of War, lists criteria for POW status:

- *that of being commanded by a person responsible for his subordinates;*
- *that of having a fixed distinctive sign recognizable at a distance;*
- *that of carrying arms openly;*
- *that of conducting their operations in accordance with the laws and customs of war.*[4]

Al-Qaeda members do not meet these criteria. There does not appear to be much structure to al-Qaeda, members try to blend in with civilians rather than "having a fixed distinctive sign recognizable from a distance," they do not carry arms openly, and killing civilians goes against the "laws and customs of war."

While lawful combatants are protected by the Third Geneva Convention, unlawful combatants are not.

Article 3 of the Third Geneva Convention

Article 3 of the Third Geneva Convention has two parts. The second part deals with treatment of the wounded. The first part details prohibited acts: "… the following acts are and shall remain prohibited at any time and in any place whatsoever with respect to the above-mentioned persons [sick, wounded, detained]:

(a) Violence to life and person, in particular murder of all kinds, mutilation, cruel treatment and torture;

(b) Taking of hostages;

(c) Outrages upon personal dignity, in particular, humiliating and degrading treatment;

(d) The passing of sentences and the carrying out of executions without previous judgment pronounced by a regularly constituted court affording all the judicial guarantees which are recognized as indispensable by civilized peoples."[5]

Determining Enemy Combatant Status

Traditionally, the military commander with the power to use deadly force with an enemy determines enemy combatant status. Because the U.S. Constitution gives the president the title and responsbility of commander in chief, the executive branch identifies enemy combatants. This includes who should be captured and detained during times of war.

Article 3 states that all prisoners of war "shall in all circumstances be treated humanely." It forbids "outrages upon personal dignity, in particular, humiliating and degrading treatment." It also prohibits sentencing or executing prisoners without judgment by a court that provides "all the judicial guarantees which are recognized as indispensable by civilized peoples."[6]

The Bush administration proposed to try cases of members of al-Qaeda, the Taliban, and other paramilitary combatants (soldiers not part of a recognized army) in special courts that would follow guidelines laid out in the Uniform Code of Military Justice (UCMJ) or the Authorization for Use of Military Force (AUMF). The AUMF was passed by Congress in the wake of September 11 to give the government increased power to fight terrorism. It specifies the following:

> *The President is authorized to use all necessary and appropriate force against those nations, organizations, or persons he determines planned, authorized, committed, or aided*

*the terrorist attacks that occurred on September 11, 2001,
or harbored such organizations or persons, in order to prevent any future acts of international terrorism against the
United States by such nations, organizations, or persons.[7]*

An American Held in America

Yaser Hamdi's father filed a habeas corpus petition
on behalf of his son. The father also claimed his son
was being held in violation of the Fifth Amendment
guarantee of due process.

The case *Hamdi v. Rumsfeld* reached the U.S. Supreme
Court in 2004. The Court concluded 8–1 that, as an
American citizen held in the United States, Hamdi had
the right to challenge his detention before a judge. As a
result, Hamdi was released from prison and allowed to
return to his native Saudi Arabia. However, he was
required to give up his American citizenship.

The Rights of Enemy Combatants

The ruling in Hamdi was later strengthened by a
similar Supreme Court decision in the case of Salim
Ahmed Hamdan. An American citizen, Hamden had
worked as a driver for Osama bin Laden, mastermind
of the September 11 attacks. Like Hamdi, Hamdan was
captured in Afghanistan and classified as an enemy

Supporters walk outside the federal courthouse in Detroit, Michigan, March 26, 2002, in support of Rabih Haddad. He and other detainees have not been granted the right to due process.

combatant. He was held for almost three years before being charged with "conspiracy to commit terrorism." In a 5–3 verdict, the Supreme Court ruled that Hamdan was protected by the Geneva Conventions. The Court also ruled that the 2001 AUMF did not give the government the right to create new courts to try such enemy combatants without the authority of Congress.

The Military Commissions Act

The ruling in *Hamdi v. Rumsfeld* concluded that it might be possible to design an "appropriately authorized and properly constituted military tribunal" where alleged enemy combatants such as Hamdi could receive due process.[8] The Military Commissions Act (MCA), passed by Congress and signed by President Bush in 2006, attempts to create such courts. Under the MCA, the accused detainee has both the right to be present at all times during his or her trial and the right to a lawyer. The defendant must have access to any evidence that might prove him or her innocent, as long as that evidence is not classified. Classified evidence is something held from the public because it may reveal information that could hurt the United States if obtained by terrorists. In addition, the accused may appeal the verdict to the District of Columbia Circuit Court and even to the U.S. Supreme Court.

Under the MCA, however, such combatants have no habeas corpus rights with which to challenge their imprisonment. The act makes providing the broadly defined "material support" and "expert

"Due process demands that a citizen held in the United States as an enemy combatant be given a meaningful opportunity to contest the factual basis for that detention before a neutral decisionmaker."[9]

—*Justice Sandra Day O'Connor in* Hamdi v. Rumsfeld

advice" to terrorists a punishable offense. It permits hearsay evidence (evidence that comes from someone else rather than from the person who directly experienced something) that cannot be forcefully challenged. The MCA also allows evidence that has been obtained through coercion, such as a forced confession. And while the MCA prohibits serious violations of the Geneva Conventions, such as torture, rape, and cruel and inhumane treatment, it also prevents individuals from protesting any violations of the Geneva Conventions standards in court.

In Favor: Constitutional Rights Not for Aliens

Former Justice Department official and current law professor John Yoo writes about the MCA and enemy status being the role of the president and Congress:

> The new law is ... a stinging rebuke to the Supreme Court. It was passed in response to the effort in ... Hamdan v. Rumsfeld to take control over terrorism policy ... an unprecedented attempt by the court to rewrite the law of war and intrude into war policy. ... Until the Supreme Court began trying to make war policy, the writ of habeas corpus had never been understood to benefit enemy prisoners of war. ... In Hamdan, the court moved to sweep aside

*decades of law and practice so as to forge a grand new role
for the courts to open their doors to enemy war prisoners. …
Thoughtful critics point out that because the enemy fights
covertly, the risk of detaining the innocent is greater. But so
is the risk of releasing the dangerous. … Until* Hamdan,
*nothing in the law of war ever suggested that enemy status
was anything but a military judgments. …this is a decision
for the president and Congress, not the courts.*[10]

Most of those determined to be unlawful combatants
are aliens. Those in favor of the MCA argue that aliens
with no immigration status do not have habeas corpus
and other Constitutional rights. Even some of those
who are otherwise opposed to the MCA have concluded
that the law denies habeas corpus rights only to aliens—
that the rights of a few are being jeopardized rather
than those of all U.S. citizens.

Opposed: The Constitution Applies to All
Speaking for MCA opponents, the ACLU states,

*The president can now—with the approval of Congress—
indefinitely hold people without charge, take away protections against horrific abuse, put people on trial based on
hearsay evidence, authorize trials that can sentence people
to death based on testimony literally beaten out of witnesses,*

and slam shut the courthouse door for habeas petitions.
Nothing could be further from the American values we all
hold in our hearts than the Military Commissions Act.[11]

This statement did not distinguish between aliens and citizens. Neither did Justice Sandra Day O'Connor in the plurality (majority) opinion in *Hamdi v. Rumsfeld*. She wrote, "All agree that, absent suspension, the writ of habeas corpus remains available to every individual detained within the United States."[12]

Despite Justice O'Connor's opinion, the day after the president signed the MCA, the government began to file court papers that would dismiss all the petitions for habeas corpus submitted by detainees at Guantanamo Bay. Approximately 400 detainees classified as "illegal enemy combatants" are jailed there. Guantanamo Bay is legally considered part of the United States. Given this, the Constitution should apply there as well. Are any or all of these detainees entitled to their day in court? If they are never tried, or if they are tried and found innocent, should they be compensated for their loss of liberty? These questions may be faced by courts in the future. Many detainees may also claim their right to a speedy and public trial by a jury of their peers.

Demonstrators protest during witness testimony at the Senate Judiciary Committee hearing titled Examining Proposals to Limit Guantanamo Detainees' Access to Habeas Corpus Review.

The defense table in the courtroom of the Commissions building at the Guantanamo Bay Naval Base in Cuba

THE RIGHT TO A SPEEDY AND PUBLIC TRIAL BY JURY

*I*n addition to habeas corpus, legal rights set forth by the Constitution and Bill of Rights include the right to a speedy and public trial by jury. The idea of a jury of one's peers first appeared in the Magna Carta, which clearly states, "No freeman shall be taken … or exiled or in any way destroyed … except by the lawful judgment of his peers or by the law of the land."[1] The right to a trial by a jury of one's fellow citizens is a major concept of the American legal system. Under the Constitution, jury service is one of the few duties required of all citizens.

The framers of the Constitution had a good reason for making citizens instead of judges decide a person's guilt or innocence: they were trying to limit the power of government over the ordinary citizen. In addition to a jury of one's peers, the Sixth Amendment specifically calls for the right to a speedy and public trial.

However, those enemy combatants deemed unlawful do not receive the same rights as ordinary U.S. citizens or even lawful enemy combatants. The president is charged with the power of determining combatant status by the U.S. Constitution. But not all international governing bodies agree with the practice of limiting the rights of detainees.

"The Trial of all Crimes, except in Cases of Impeachment, shall be by Jury."[2]

—*Article 3, Section 2 U.S. Constitution*

"In all criminal prosecutions, the accused shall enjoy the right to a speedy and public trial by an impartial jury … and to be informed of the nature and cause of the accusation; to be confronted with the witnesses against him; to have compulsory process for obtaining witnesses in his favor, and to have the Assistance of Counsel for his defen[s]e."[3]

—*Amendment VI U.S. Constitution*

According to the Council of Europe, the political body that governs the European Union, the concept of unlawful enemy combatant is "unknown in international law and corresponds to no legal status."[4]

The Fate of Long-term Detainees

While the Council of Europe finds no legal status for unlawful enemy combatants, the U.S. government continues under the idea that the term *unlawful enemy combatant* is necessary to fight America's war on terror. Such enemies could be

---

The Geneva Convention

Adopted August 12, 1949, the Geneva Convention has 143 articles divided into six parts:
Part I: General Provisions
Part II: General Protection of Prisoners of War
Part III: Captivity
Part IV: Termination of Captivity
Part V: Information Bureaus and Relief Societies
Part VI: Execution of the Convention
Article 13 addresses the treatment of prisoners of war:

Prisoners of war must at all times be humanely treated. Any unlawful act or omission by the Detaining Power causing death or seriously endangering the health of a prisoner of war in its custody is prohibited, and will be regarded as a serious breach of the present Convention. In particular, no prisoner of war may be subjected to physical mutilation or to medical or scientific experiments of any kind which are not justified by the medical, dental or hospital treatment of the prisoner concerned and carried out in his interest.

Likewise, prisoners of war must at all times be protected, particularly against acts of violence or intimidation and against insults and public curiosity.

Measures of reprisal against prisoners of war are prohibited.[5]

held indefinitely and without charges.
Several hundred of those captured in
Afghanistan and now detained at
Guantanamo Bay have been held for
almost five years, many without any
charges being made against them. If
they were ever brought to trial, it
would be in a military court. The
government claims the detentions are
proper since alien unlawful enemy
combatants have no legal rights.
Critics respond that all prisoners of
war should be subject to the Geneva Conventions. They
concede, however, that a U.S. court might rule that the
Geneva Conventions do not cover an alien tried by a
military court in the United States. If these alien
combatants were convicted in such a trial, they could
only appeal their convictions to the president currently
in office. This could be the same person who
designated them "unlawful combatants" and ordered
their trial.

Council of Europe

Founded in 1949, the
Council of Europe has 47
member countries. The
Council of Europe's mission
is "to develop throughout
Europe common and dem-
ocratic principles based on
the European Convention
on Human Rights and other
reference texts on the
protection of individuals."[6]

For detainees, perhaps more frightening than being
held indefinitely and without formal charges is the
possibility of being abused while detained. This has
become a reality for some prisoners. The Eighth

Detainees at Guantanamo (as of December 31, 2006)

Number of detainees who have been held: 773

Detainees released or transferred: 377

Detainees released who were sent home: 150

Detainees remaining in custody: 396

Detainees expected to face military trial: 50–70[7]

Amendment addresses cruel and unusual punishment—a topic at the forefront for the U.S. military and detainees at Guantanamo Bay and at Abu Ghraib, a former prison in Iraq that became the focus of American media attention in 2004.

Detainees, including Taliban and al-Qaeda suspects, dressed in orange, sit in a holding area under the watchful eyes of military police at Guantanamo Bay, Cuba.

U.S. troops at Abu Ghraib prison in Iraq in 2003

The Eighth Amendment

When creating the Constitution, the framers wanted to ensure that the new U.S. government would not be allowed to commit horrible acts against citizens when they were charged with a crime. This often had been the case in England.

In the seventeenth century, for example, the king could imprison persons accused of a crime for as long as he wanted without a trial. The bail was set so high that the accused could not afford to pay it. The founding fathers wanted to avoid the types of cruel and unusual punishments that were commonplace in England, such as being burnt alive. The issue of torture is still very much being debated all these years later.

What Is Torture?

Torture is often described as cruel and unusual punishment, but what does that phrase mean? The United Nations Convention against Torture and Other Cruel, Inhuman or Degrading Treatment or Punishment, signed by the United States, defines torture as "severe pain or suffering, whether physical or mental," inflicted as punishment or to force a person to reveal information.[1]

U.S. Supreme Court Justice William Brennan expanded the definition of cruel and unusual punishments to include those that are "degrading to human dignity," such as torture, which is intended to break the will of the subject; "inflicted in a

"Excessive bail shall not be required, nor excessive fines imposed, nor cruel and unusual punishments inflicted."[2]

—Amendment VIII
U.S. Constitution

wholly arbitrary fashion;" "clearly and totally rejected throughout society;" and "patently unnecessary."[3]

One example of torture that is often mentioned is "waterboarding." This procedure makes prisoners feel like they are drowning. U.S. Vice President Dick Cheney admits that American interrogators have used waterboarding on captured terrorist suspects. The Geneva Conventions forbid torture of prisoners of war. However, the Bush administration claims that the Geneva Conventions do not apply to those classified as unlawful enemy combatants, including al-Qaeda.

In Favor: Ticking Time Bombs

Some people believe a case can be

Torture or Humane Treatment?

U.S. citizen and alleged terrorist Jose Padilla was held in solitary confinement in the United States without formal charges for more than three years. He slept on a steel platform without a mattress. According to Padilla's lawyer, his Koran was taken from him "as part of an interrogation plan" that included hooding, stress positions, assaults, and threats of execution.[4] When removed from his cell, Padilla was shackled, blindfolded, and forced to wear noise-blocking earphones and light-blocking goggles.

Padilla's lawyers claimed that his treatment resulted in post-traumatic stress syndrome. They said that this condition made Padilla unable to assist in his own defense. A Pentagon spokesman strongly denied the charge that Padilla had been tortured, stating, "Padilla's conditions of confinement were humane and designed to ensure his safety and security."[5]

Padilla was convicted in August 2007 on charges of terrorism conspiracy.

made for permitting torture in instances of "ticking time bombs." These are cases in which a captured terrorist knows of a specific, immediate, and serious threat to the public but refuses to give any information about it. In such instances, some believe that a judge should have the legal right to allow torture that would force the terrorist to reveal the information. The benefit of torture in such instances might seem obvious—harm to one could ultimately save many more lives if that one person provided information that would prevent a terrorist attack. However, a lawyer trying to make a case in court would have to prove that the methods used were not cruel and unusual punishments as prohibited by the Eighth Amendment.

When the United States first proposed to try unlawful enemy combatants in military courts in 2002, torture was ruled out as a way of questioning prisoners. The government defines torture as an unusual punishment as not just "moderate and fleeting pain," but that torture "must be equivalent in intensity to the

Cruel and Unusual Punishment

While the term *cruel and unusual punishment* is common, there is no single definition of it that is accepted worldwide. Rather, any punishment that is inhumane or that violates basic human dignity may be considered "cruel and unusual." However, opinions on the matter can vary from person to person, especially given the reason for the punishment.

pain accompanying serious physical injury, such as organ failure, impairment of bodily function, or even death."[6] Almost two years later, however, a new definition of torture was being put into practice in places other than Guantanamo. The name Abu Ghraib was soon to become a household word.

Abu Ghraib

Abu Ghraib was a prison in Iraq where up to 7,000 insurgents, or rebels, were held. In January 2004, Sergeant Joseph Darby gave the U.S. Army Criminal Investigation Command photographs showing prisoner abuse at Abu Ghraib. The photographs quickly became public, appearing on television news, the Internet, and newspapers. The images showed prisoners being paraded nude, threatened by dogs, and in various humiliating positions. While the Geneva Convention prohibits such treatment of detainees as torture, many of these techniques had been approved at the highest levels of the Pentagon. There were several investigations into the matter. Nine U.S. soldiers were tried and convicted in the scandal.

Detainee Treatment Act of 2005

Senator John McCain took action to ensure that the

U.S. Army Sergeant Joseph Darby, right, receives a special Profile in Courage Award from Caroline Kennedy and Senator Edward M. Kennedy.

events at Abu Ghraib would not be repeated. As a former prisoner of war, McCain had been tortured by the North Vietnamese during the Vietnam War. To outlaw torture of terrorism suspects, McCain introduced a bill that became known as the Detainee Treatment Act (DTA) of 2005. The DTA limited interrogation techniques to those listed in the Army's

U.S. Senator John McCain was a prisoner for more than five years during the Vietnam War. He is an advocate for the fair treatment of detainees.

field manual on interrogation. This work, revised in 2005, forbade such acts as stripping prisoners; forcing them to stand, sit, or kneel in abnormal positions for long periods; depriving them of food and normal sleep; or using police dogs to frighten them.

In December 2006, the *New York Times* reported that to avoid the new law, the Pentagon had rewritten the *Army Field Manual.* Ten pages in the interrogation section of the revision are now classified. Army officers said the reason for secrecy was to prevent detainees from learning how to counter the interrogation techniques described in these pages. Some people believe that this was done to get around the act by detailing methods of torture that would then be allowed under the act.

COERCION OR TORTURE?

The Military Commissions Act (MCA) allows evidence that has been obtained through coercion to be used in court, as long as a judge rules that it is reliable. While coercion and torture may overlap, a person who is coerced can still make a rational decision. A person being tortured, however, loses the ability to make such a rational decision. Under the MCA, coerced statements obtained since the DTA went into effect on December 30, 2005, are banned if they are the

"September 11, 2001, caused many to reflect upon the fundamental values on which this country was founded: freedom of speech, respect for human dignity, freedom of religion, justice for all, tolerance. It is imperative that the United States stand for the principles of unalienable, universal rights. Otherwise, those who wage war on human rights will have won the battle against freedom. Amnesty International is concerned the 'war on terror' not become an excuse to deny human rights."[7]

—*Amnesty International*

result of what can be called cruel, inhuman, or degrading treatment under the Constitution. The MCA protects classified interrogation methods from being made public. Human rights attorney Joanne Mariner notes that without knowing what interrogation techniques are used by the U.S. military and the Central Intelligence Agency, it seems unlikely that the methods will be questioned as improper.

Returning to the unlawful enemy combatants being held by the U.S. military at Guantanamo and other locations, there are many questions regarding their fate and the methods used to gather evidence against them. The fight for civil liberties has been ongoing for centuries. Since the attacks of September 11, 2001, and the war on terror that has followed, there has been a great deal of focus on the subject of civil liberties in the United States. Clearly, there are many differing viewpoints. With the First Amendment, everyone is free to voice their opinions.

Invoking their rights to free speech and to assemble peacefully, thousands of people gathered in San Francisco, California, in 2002 to protest the war in Iraq.

TIMELINE

1215	1689	1776
Magna Carta is signed by King John of England June 15.	On December 16, Parliament passes a Declaration of Rights, now known as the Bill of Rights, proclaiming new civil liberties.	On July 4, the American Declaration of Independence lists the lack of civil rights as one complaint against the English monarchy.

1861	1866	1917
President Lincoln suspends habeas corpus in parts of the Union April 27.	On April 3, in *Ex Parte Milligan,* Supreme Court rules 9–0 that Lincoln acted illegally in suspending habeas corpus during Civil War.	U.S. Congress passes the Espionage Act June 15.

1789

France makes official its Declaration of the Rights of Man and of the Citizen August 27.

1791

First ten amendments become part of the U.S. Constitution December 15.

1798

President John Adams signs the Sedition Act July 14.

1918

U.S. Congress passes the Sedition Act as amendment to Espionage Act May 16.

1919

On March 3, Supreme Court upholds by 9–0 *Schenck v. United States*, restricting free speech.

1942

By Executive Order 9066, on February 19, President Franklin D. Roosevelt detains over 110,000 Japanese-Americans in the United States.

TIMELINE

1942	1944	1949
On July 31, the Supreme Court defines "unlawful enemy combatant" in *Ex Parte Quirin*, ruling them "not entitled to the status of prisoner of war."	In *Korematsu v. U.S.*, on December 18, Fred Korematsu loses Supreme Court challenge to Executive Order 9066.	The Third Geneva Convention, which pertains to the treatment of prisoners of war, is adopted August 12.

2001	2001	2004
United States begins war on Afghanistan with air strikes against Taliban and al-Qaeda forces October 7.	President Bush signs the USA Patriot Act October 26.	In January, Sergeant Joseph Darby gives U.S. authorities photographs showing prisoner torture in Abu Ghraib prison in Iraq.

1983

Fred Korematsu's conviction for violating Executive Order 9066 is voided November 10.

2001

On September 11, terrorists attack the United States, killing almost 3,000 people.

2001

On September 18, President Bush signs the Authorization for Use of Military Force, giving him increased powers to fight terrorism.

2004

On June 28, Supreme Court rules that foreign nationals detained at Guantanamo Bay may challenge their detainment in U.S. federal courts.

2005

Detainee Treatment Act goes into effect December 30.

2006

The Military Commissions Act is signed by President Bush October 17 to create special courts in which defendants have no habeas corpus rights.

Essential Facts

At Issue

Opposed

❖ It is not patriotic to suspend civil liberties. A democracy must remain democratic, even during times of war.

❖ The USA Patriot Act gives the president too much power for a democratic nation.

In Favor

❖ In wartime, the safety of the nation must come before the safety of the individual.

❖ The USA Patriot Act allows the president to act quickly against terrorism to maintain and increase the security of the nation.

Critical Dates

1215
King John signed the Magna Carta, giving some of his power to a council of barons that later became England's Parliament.

1689
The English Parliament passed the Bill of Rights that proclaimed new civil liberties.

1776
The Declaration of Independence declared that the British were violating the colonists' civil liberties.

1791
The Bill of Rights was added to the U.S. Constitution.

1798
John Adams signed the Alien Enemies Act, the Alien Friends Act, the Naturalization Act, and the Sedition Act in response to a fear of French immigrants. He became the first U.S. president to limit civil liberties.

1861
Abraham Lincoln used his presidential power to suspend habeas corpus during the Civil War.

1942

Woodrow Wilson became the third president to limit civil liberties by signing Executive Order 9066, resulting in the detainment of over 110,000 Japanese-Americans in the United States during World War II.

2001

On September 11, terrorists attacked the United States. President Bush signed the Authorization for Use of Military Force, giving him increased powers to fight terrorism. The United States began the war on Afghanistan. President Bush signed the USA Patriot Act.

2004

Army Sargeant Joseph Darby gave authorities photographs showing prisoner torture in Abu Ghraib prison in Iraq. U.S. Supreme Court ruled that foreign nationals detained at Guantanamo Bay may challenge their detainment in U.S. federal courts.

Quotes

Opposed

"The president can now—with the approval of Congress—indefinitely hold people without charge, take away protections against horrific abuse, put people on trial based on hearsay evidence, authorize trials that can sentence people to death based on testimony literally beaten out of witnesses, and slam shut the courthouse door for habeas petitions. Nothing could be further from the American values we all hold in our hearts than the Military Commissions Act."—*ACLU*

In Favor

"The law allows our intelligence and law enforcement officials to continue to share information. It allows them to continue to use tools against terrorists that they used against—that they use against drug dealers and other criminals. It will improve our nation's security while we safeguard the civil liberties of our people. The legislation strengthens the Justice Department so it can better detect and disrupt terrorist threats. And the bill gives law enforcement new tools to combat threats to our citizens from international terrorists to local drug dealers."—
President George W. Bush at the signing of the USA Patriot Improvement and Reauthorization Act of 2005

ADDITIONAL RESOURCES

SELECT BIBLIOGRAPHY

Hudson, David. *The Bill of Rights: The First Ten Amendments to the Constitution.* Springfield, NJ: Enslow, 2002.

Levy, Debbie. *Civil Liberties.* San Diego: Lucent, 1999.

Nardo, Don. *The Bill of Rights.* San Diego: Greenhaven, 1997.

Torr, James D., ed. *Civil Liberties.* Farmington Hills, MI: Greenhaven, 2003.

Understanding Terrorism Cases: The Role of Federal Courts in Balancing Liberties and Safety. 3 Jan. 2007 <http://www.uscourts.gov/outreach/topics/habeascorpus_landmark.htm>.

FURTHER READING

Freedman, Russell. *In Defense of Liberty: The Story of America's Bill of Rights.* New York: Holiday House, 2003.

Krull, Kathleen. *A Kid's Guide to America's Bill of Rights: Curfews, Censorship, and the 100-Pound Giant.* New York: Avon, 1999.

Zacharias, Gary and Jared Zacharias, eds. *Bill of Rights (At Issue in History series).* San Diego: Greenhaven, 2002.

Web Links

To learn more about civil liberties, visit ABDO Publishing Company on the World Wide Web at **www.abdopublishing.com**. Web sites about civil liberties are featured on our Book Links page. These links are routinely monitored and updated to provide the most current information available.

Places to Visit

Independence Hall, Philadelphia
Chestnut Street, between Fifth and Sixth Streets, Philadelphia, PA 19106
877-444-6777
www.ushistory.org/tour/tour_indhall.htm
Part of the Independence National Historic Park, which includes the site where the Constitution was written, the Liberty Bell, and the National Constitutional Center.

National Archives Building
700 Pennsylvania Avenue NW, Washington, DC 20408
202-357-5000
www.archives.gov/dc-metro/washington/
Rotunda for the Charters of Freedom contains all four pages of the Constitution. Learning Center provides hands-on activities and opportunities for on-line exploration.

Supreme Court of the United States
One First Street NE, Washington, DC 20543
202-479-3000
www.supremecourtus.gov
The Court convenes beginning the first Monday in October and continues in session until all its cases are heard. Oral arguments on Mondays, Tuesdays, and Wednesdays of the first two weeks of each month can be heard by visitors in their entirety or as part of a short tour.

GLOSSARY

Authorization for Use of Military Force (AUMF, 2001)
A joint resolution of Congress that authorized the president to use "all necessary and appropriate forces" against those he determined responsible for the attacks of September 11, 2001, or who harbored such persons.

bail
An amount of money someone in jail pays to the court as a condition of being released. It is used to guarantee that the person will not leave town or disappear before his or her trial begins.

bill of rights
A list of civil liberties protected by a nation's laws.

civil liberties
Individual freedoms, such as freedom of speech, that are protected under a nation's laws.

coercion
The use of physical or psychological tactics to force someone to give up information.

detainee
Someone held in prison because he or she is suspected of being a terrorist or of helping terrorists.

Detainee Treatment Act
A law passed by U.S. Congress in 2005 that prohibits inhumane treatment of detainees by limiting interrogation techniques to those described in the Army's field manual on interrogation.

due process
The legal concept that no person should be deprived of his or her life, liberty, or property without the protection of that person's legal rights.

Geneva Conventions
A series of international agreements that govern the treatment of wounded, sick, prisoners, and other victims of war.

habeas corpus
Latin for "you have the body," the legal concept that any person arrested for a crime must be brought before a judge and charged with a crime before being put on trial.

Magna Carta
An agreement made in the year 1215 between King John of England and a group of barons in which the king gave up some powers to his noble subjects.

Military Commissions Act (2006)
An act that created special courts to try "alien unlawful enemy combatants" in which these defendants lack habeas corpus rights.

terrorism
The unlawful use of violent or destructive acts in order to attempt to force a government or society to meet political, religious, or ideological objectives.

torture
As defined by the Geneva Conventions, "severe pain or suffering, whether physical or mental" that is inflicted either as punishment or to force a person to reveal information.

unlawful enemy combatant
A category of combatant defined in *Ex Parte Quirin* (1942) as one "who without uniform comes secretly through the lines for the purpose of waging war," but later broadened by the Military Commissions Act to include anyone so designated by the president of the United States.

USA Patriot Act
A law passed by Congress immediately after the events of September 11, 2001, that gave the president expanded powers to fight terrorism.

SOURCE NOTES

Chapter 1. Government Power and Civil Liberties
1. Declaration of Independence. 2 July 2007.
2. U.S. Constitution, amend. 5. 2 July 2007.
3. U.S. Constitution, amend. 6. 2 July 2007.
4. David Shavin. "On the Athenian Constitution by Solon of Athens." *Schillerinstitute.org.* 2001. 20 Nov. 2006. <http://www.schillerinstitute.org/fid_91-96/fid_932_solon.htm?
5. Aristotle. *Politics.* Whitefish, MT: Kessinger Publishing, 2004. 85.

Chapter 2. A Brief History of Civil Liberties: 1215–1789
1. "British Library treasures in full: Magna Carta" (English translation). 2 July 2007 <http://www.bl.uk/treasures/magnacarta/translation.html>.
2. "Parliament's role." 31 May 2007. *UK Parliament.* 2 July 2007 <http://www.parliament.uk/about/how/role.cfm>.
3. George Mason, "Declaration of Rights." June 12, 1776. *The Founders' Constitution.* Eds. Philip B. Kurland and Ralph L. Lerner. Chicago: University of Chicago/Liberty Fund, 8 Nov. 2006 <http://presspubs.uchicago.edu/founders/documents/bill_of_rightss2.html>.
4. "Declaration of Independence: A History." *The National Archives Experience.* U.S. National Archives and Records Administration. 2 July 2007 <http://www.archives.gov/national-archives-experience/charters/declaration_history.html>.

Chapter 3. Is a Bill of Rights Necessary?
1. Alexander Hamilton. "The Federalist Papers, #84, 575–81" 28 May 1788. *The Founders' Constitution.* Eds. Philip B. Kurland and Ralph L. Lerner. 1987. Chicago: U of Chicago P/Liberty Fund. 4 Jan. 2007 <http://press-pubs.uchicago.edu/founders/documents/bill_of_rightss7.html>.
2. Robert Yates. "To the citizens of New York." (Anti-Federalist Papers: Brutus 2) 1 Nov. 1787. *Constitution Society.* 22 Mar. 2007 <http://www.constitution.org/afp/brutus02.htm>.
3. George Mason. "Objections to the Proposed Constitution." *The American Constitution, For and Against: The Federalist and Anti-Federalist Papers.* Ed. J.R. Pole. New York: Farrar, Straus & Giroux, 1987. 28.
4. Thomas Jefferson. "Letter of December 20, 1787, to James Madison." *The Life and Selected Writings of Thomas Jefferson.* Eds. Adrienne Koch and William Peden. New York: Random House, 1944. 462.
5. Hadley Arkes. "A Reconsideration of the Original Case against the Bill of Rights," *TeachingAmericanHistory.org.* Ashbrook Center for Public Affairs at Ashland University. 2006, 4 Jan. 2007 <http://teachingamericanhistory.org/seminars/2004/arkes.html>.

6. Declaration of the Rights of Man and the Citizen, 1789. *Office of the French President.* 2 July 2007 <http://www.elysee.fr/elysee/anglais/the_institutions/founding_texts/the_declaration_of_the_human_rights/the_declaration_of_the_human_rights.20240.html>.

Chapter 4. Limiting Civil Liberties for National Security
1. The Sedition Act of 1798, Stats at Large of USA (1798), Fifth Congress, Vol. 1, 1845.
2. U.S. Constitution, art. 1, sec. 9. 2 July 2007.
3. "The Charters of Freedom: A New World is at Hand." The National Archives Experience. U.S. National Archives and Records Administration. 2 July 2007 <http://www.archives.gov/national-archives-experience/charters/charters_of_freedom_7.html>.
4. Learned Hand. "I Am an American Day." Central Park, New York, 21 May 1944. *National Association of Criminal Defense Lawyers E-News.* 2 July 2007 <http://www.nacdl.org/_852566CF0070A126.nsf/0/B9CC1CBED08C01808 5256C0500835099?Open>.
5. "Primary Documents: U.S. Espionage Act, 15 June 1917." FirstWorldWar.com. 5 May 2002. *FirstWorldWar.com.* 11 March 2007. <http://www.firstworldwar.com/source/espionageact.htm>.
6. Sedition Act of 1918, 16 May 1918. Stat. 40.353.
7. *Schenck v. U.S.*, No. 249 U.S. 47, Supreme Ct of the US, 3 March 1919.
8. "The Anti-war Speech That Earned Eugene Debs 10 Years in Prison." *The Memory Hole.* 23 Oct. 2006. 4 Jan. 2007. <http://www.thememoryhole.org/war/debs-speech.htm>
9. "Milton Eisenhower Justifies the Internment of Japanese Americans." *History Matters: The U.S. Survey Course on the Web.* 31 March 2006, 4 Jan. 2007. <http://historymatters.gmu.edu/d/5153>
10. *Korematsu v. U.S.*, No. 323 U.S. 214, Supreme Ct of the US, 18 Dec. 1944.
11. U.S. Department of Justice. "The USA Patriot Act: Preserving Life and Liberty." 2 July 2007 <http://www.lifeandliberty.gov/what_is_the_patriot_act.pdf>.

Chapter 5. The First Amendment
1. U.S. Constitution, amend 1. 2 July 2007 <http://www.archives.gov/national-archives-experience/charters/bill_of_rights_transcript.html>.
2. Kate Randall. "U.S. Judge Orders Open Hearing for Detained Muslim Cleric." WSWS.org. 5 April 2002, 2 July 2007 <http://www.wsws.org/articles/2002/apr2002/hadd-a05.shtml>.
3. Thomas Jefferson. Letter to Col. Edward Carrington. 16 January 1787. *Bartlett's Familiar Quotations.* Ed. Emily Morrison Beck. Boston: Little, Brown, 1968. 471a.
4. *Tinker v. Des Moines Independent Community School District*, No. 393 U.S. 503, Supreme Ct. of the US, 24 Feb. 1969.
5. George W. Bush. "Address to a Joint Session of Congress and the American People." 20 Sept. 2001. *WhiteHouse.gov.* 7 Jan. 2007 <http://www.whitehouse.gov/news/releases/2001/09/20010920-8.html>.

SOURCE NOTES CONTINUED

6. Carol D. Leonnig, "Desecration of Koran Had Been Reported Before." *Washington Post,* 18 May 2005: A12. 4 January 2007 <http://www.washingtonpost. com/wp-dyn/content/article/2005/05/17/AR2005051701315_pf.html>.
7. George W. Bush. "Statement to reporters during a meeting with U.N. Secretary General Kofi Annan." Oval Office, Washington, D.C. 13 Nov. 2002 <http://www.whitehouse.gov/infocus/ramadan/islam.html>.

Chapter 6. The Fourth Amendment
1. U.S. Constitution, amend 4. 2 July 2007.
2. Ibid.
3. "Warrantless Mail Searches May Be Allowed." *MSNBC.com.* 5 Jan. 2007. 7 Jan. 2007 <http://www.msnbc.msn.com/id/16472777>.
4. Heather Mac Donald, "In Defense of the Patriot Act" *Washington Post.* 24 Aug. 2003. 4 Jan. 2007 <http://www.manhattan-institute.org/html/_washpost-patriot_act.htm>.
5. Ann Beeson and Jameel Jaffer. "Unpatriotic Acts: The FBI's Power to Rifle through Your Records and Personal Belongings without Telling You." New York: American Civil Liberties Union, 2003. 4 Jan. 2007 <http://www.aclu. org/safefree/resources/16813pub20030730.html>.
6. Brian T. Yeh and Charles Doyle. "USA Patriot Improvement and Reauthorizaton Act of 2005: A Legal Analysis." Washington, D.C.: Congressional Research Service, 2006. CRS-6. 2 July 2007 <http://www.fas. org/sgp/crs/intel/RL33332.pdf>.
7. *Olmstead v. U.S.*, No. 277 U.S. 438, Supreme Ct. of the US, 9 April 1928.

Chapter 7. Habeas Corpus and Due Process
1. U.S. Constitution, art. 1, sec. 9. 2 July 2007.
2. U.S. Constitution, amend 5. 2 July 2007.
3. Ex Parte Quirin, No. 317 US 1, Supreme Ct. of the US, 31 July 1942.
4. Geneva Convention Relative to the Treatment of Prisoners of War, art. 4. Office of the UN High Commissioner for Human Rights. 21 October 1950. 4 January 2007 <http://www.unhchr.ch/html/menu3/b/91.htm>.
5. Geneva Convention Relative to the Treatment of Prisoners of War, art. 3. Office of the UN High Commissioner for Human Rights. 21 October 1950. 4 Jan. 2007 <http://www.unhchr.ch/html/menu3/b/91.htm>.
6. Ibid.
7. Authorization for Use of Military Force. Pub. L. 107-40. 18 Sept. 2001.
8. Hamdi v. Rumsfeld, No. 542 US 507, Supreme Ct. of the US, 28 June 2004.
9. Ibid.
10. John Yoo. "Sending a Message Congress to Courts: Get out of the War on Terror." *WSJ.com Opinion Journal.* 19 October 2006, 4 Jan. 2007 <http://www.opinionjournal.com/editorial/feature.html?id=110009113>.
11. "President Signs Un-American Military Commissions Act, ACLU Says New

Law Undermines Due Process and the Rule of Law." 17 Oct. 2006. 4 Jan. 2007
<http://www.aclu.org/safefree/detention/27091prs20061017.
html>.
12. *Hamdi v. Rumsfeld*, No. 542 US 507, Supreme Ct. of the US, 28 June 2004.

Chapter 8. The Right to a Speedy and Public Trial by Jury
1. "British Library treasures in full: Magna Carta" (English translation). 2 July
2007 <http://www.bl.uk/treasures/magnacarta/translation.html>.
2. U.S. Constitution, art. 3, sec. 2. 2 July 2007.
3. U.S. Constitution, amend 6. 2 July 2007.
4. Parliamentary Assembly, Council of Europe, Committee on Legal Affairs and
Human Rights. "Rights of persons held in the custody of the United States in
Afghanistan or Guantanamo Bay," 26 May 2003. 4 Jan. 2007 <http://assembly.
coe.int/main.asp?Link=/documents/workingdocs/doc03/edoc9817.htm>.
5. Geneva Convention Relative to the Treatment of Prisoners of War, art. 4.
Office of the High Commissioner for Human Rights. 21 Oct. 1950, 11 Mar.
2007 <http://www.unhchr.ch/html/menu3/b/91.htm>.
6. Council of Europe. "About the Council of Europe." 2 July 2007
<http://www.coe.int/T/e/Com/about_coe/>.
7. Tim Golden, "For Guantanamo Review Boards, Limits Abound," New York
Times 31 December 2006: A1. 2 July 2007 <http://www.nytimes.com/
2006/12/31/us/31gitmo.html?ex=1325221200&en=1faefe91f8f0c2a8&ei=5088&
partner=rssnyt&emc=rss>.

Chapter 9. The Eighth Amendment
1. Convention against Torture and Other Cruel, Inhuman or Degrading
Treatment or Punishment, art. 1. Office of the High Commissioner for Human
Rights. 10 Dec. 1984, 3 July 2007 <http://www.unhchr.ch/html/menu3/
b/h_cat39.htm >.
2. U.S. Constitution, amend 8. 2 July 2007.
3. *Furman v. Georgia*, No. 408 US 238, Supreme Ct. of the US, 29 June 1972.
4. Deborah Sontag, "Videotape Offers a Window into a Terror Suspect's
Isolation," *New York Times.* 4 December 2006: A1.
5. Quoted in Sontag, A 22. <http://www.nytimes.com/2006/12/04/us/04detain
.html?ex=1322888400&en=accb01df2436f791&ei=5090&partner=rssuser>.
6. "Memo Offered Justification for Use of Torture," *Washington Post.* 8 June 2004:
A01. <http://www.washingtonpost.com/wp-dyn/articles/A23373-2004Jun7.
html>.
7. Amnesty International USA. "The 'War on Terror' Must Not Be an Excuse to
Deny Human Rights" 2007, 2 July 2007 <http://www.amnestyusa.org/Our_
Issues/War_on_Terror/page.do?id=1021007&n1=3&n2=821>.
8. "USA Patriot Act." *WhiteHouse.gov.* 9 Mar. 2006, 2 July 2007
<http://www.whitehouse.gov/infocus/patriotact/>.

INDEX

ABOUT THE AUTHOR

Scott Gillam is a former English teacher and editor of social studies and language arts textbooks. He is a graduate of Haverford College, has a master's degree from the University of Pennsylvania, and served as an education officer with the Peace Corps in Kenya. He is also the author of *Discrimination: Prejudice in Action* and *Top Careers in Two Years: Food, Agriculture, and Natural Resources.*

PHOTO CREDITS